This down-to-earth book is a giant parish booster shot! Matthew Halbach provides an abundance of commonsense ideas for opening doorways to God's liberating mercy. Bolstered by the healing words of Pope Francis, this "must-read" book is ideal for parish renewal, reassessment, and rebirth.

GERARD F. BAUMBACH, ED.D.,
Professor Emeritus, Institute for Church Life, Director Emeritus of the Echo Program, University of Notre Dame

In this first-rate publication Matthew Halbach captures the identity Pope Francis inspires all of us to become—missionary disciples. As faithful disciples we absorb the endless mercy of the Master in personal companionship. The mission field to be cultivated is located in the midst of fellow parishioners. Dr. Halbach provides key insights as to how to bring the transforming news of mercy to those ever so close who hunger and thirst for it.

BISHOP RICHARD PATES,
Bishop of Des Moines

Halbach casts wide a vision of the heart of mercy—theologically engaging the human experience and providing meaningful reflections and practical steps for parishes that take seriously the evangelizing mission of the gospel.

DIANE LAMPITT, M.ED.,
VP Product Management Religion, Wm. II. Sadlier

Grounded in Pope Francis' vision of mercy, this book is an invitation to the parish community to share the vision. Through personal stories, scriptural wisdom, and Church teaching, the reader is gently immersed into the meaning and scope of mercy. Parish communities will be enlightened and encouraged to be merciful in the ministerial and organizational objectives of the parish.

MARYLIN KRAVATZ-TOOLAN, PH.D.,
Director of the Online Institute for Religious Studies and Education Ministry, Felician University

In warm and engaging fashion, Matthew Halbach opens up the call to mercy and illustrates how it works in our personal lives as well as in the life of a parish. Woven throughout are illustrations of mercy taken from personal encounters in his own life. The book is insightful for those reading it on their own as well as leaders seeking particular ways to make mercy central to the parish mission and practice. Thought-provoking questions at the end of each chapter will most certainly spark personal reflection as well as group discussion. Of particular interest is his description of key actions and attitudes of spiritual accompaniment. These take the concept of mercy out of the merely theoretical and make its practice accessible and applicable to all facets of one's life and faith.

KATHY HENDRICKS
National Religion Consultant for Wm. H. Sadlier and author of **The Spirituality of Parenting** *and* **Forming Faith in Families**

✠ BECOMING

a PARISH

of MERCY

A New Vision for Total Parish Evangelization

MATTHEW W. HALBACH, PH.D.

**TWENTY-THIRD
PUBLICATIONS**

twentythirdpublications.com

Texts from Pope Francis,
© Liberia Editrice Vaticana,
used with permission.

TWENTY-THIRD PUBLICATIONS
1 Montauk Avenue, Suite 200, New London, CT 06320
(860) 437-3012 » (800) 321-0411 » www.twentythirdpublications.com

ISBN: 978-1-62785-159-6
Library of Congress Catalog Card Number: 2015957205
Printed in the U.S.A.

CONTENTS

Introduction

God Draws Straight
with Crooked Lines

M y parents divorced when I was about nine years old. Around this time, I remember sitting in my religious education class listening to the teacher speak about God's mercy. One thing she said really stuck with me: that *God draws straight with crooked lines*. The pain and confusion of my parents' divorce still fresh in my mind, I wanted more than anything to believe those words. Looking back after twenty-eight years, I have come to believe.

The relationships we share today as a post-divorce family are substantially different from before, as you can imagine. In some respects, the divorce precipitated positive changes, such as the deepening of faith and renewed appreciation for one another. These changes were made possible primarily through individual family members returning to the sacraments of reconciliation and Eucharist and choosing to share the graces they've received with each other. Mercy, more than anything else, has been the way in which God has made straight the "crookedness" in my family. Believe me, God can draw straight with crooked lines.

My own post-divorce healing was helped along by my good friend Fr. Mike Phillips. He is more like a surrogate father than a pastor. He has been such a positive and formative presence in my life over the years that my wife, Stacy, and I decided to name our first child after him. Though retired now and living the "life of Riley," Father Mike continues to be a presence in my family's life. He comes over for dinner now and then, and my kids run to see and hug their "Funcle Mike," which is the name you get when you combine the words "father" and "uncle." Again, God draws straight with crooked lines, and Father Mike has been like a marvelous "pen" in the merciful Father's hand.

Thinking back on the words of my religious education teacher—and reflecting on what Pope Francis has been saying and writing with regard to mercy—I was inspired to write this book. Francis is helping the Church to make straight its own "crooked lines" by offering himself as a companion to others. He is a "people's pope," choosing to walk alongside those he shepherds, wanting to understand their hopes and fears, and willing to walk in their shoes for a while if it means bringing them closer to Christ. In other words, Francis is a pope who knows how to accompany others.

Accompaniment, though, is not just the business of popes or priests like Father Mike; accompaniment is how we live as Church, it's how we evangelize and show mercy to others. As Francis stated in his exhortation, *Evangelii Gaudium* (EG), "The Joy of the Gospel":

> *The Church will have to initiate everyone—priests, religious and laity—into this "art of accompaniment" which teaches us to remove our sandals before the sacred ground of the other (cf. Ex 3:5). The pace of this accompaniment must be steady and reassuring, reflecting our closeness and our compassionate gaze which also heals, liberates and encourages growth in the Christian life.* (EG, NO. 169)

The heart of the gospels is mercy. So, how we share the gospel message ought to be mercy-full. And it begins with knowing that evangelization is not just about having the right resources, programs, and events. It's about people—people caring for people, accompanying them, and being examples of God's mercy to others.

God is the Great Companion— God "draws straight with

crooked lines." And the instrument—the "pen"—is accompaniment. God accompanies us around life's every twist and turn. God is also mercy itself. Therefore, when God extends mercy to us, God extends himself. Taking our cue from this, to be a more merciful people—a more merciful church—we must, like God, extend ourselves to others. And we do this through the work of accompaniment.

Making disciples is a widely talked about topic today. Disciples are a people of accompaniment. In fact, accompaniment describes both the purpose and the life of the disciple: disciples are people who allow God to accompany them, and they, in turn, accompany others. Disciples are called to make the presence of Christ manifest in their own lives, according to the words of Scripture: "and they shall name him Emmanuel, which means 'God is with us'" (Mt 1:23; cf. Is 7:14). Through the Church—and through you and me, personally—God, the Great Companion, seeks to accompany his people: to draw straight their crooked lines.

Mercy being the *character* of evangelization, Pope Francis is encouraging the Church today to consider accompaniment as the way we evangelize. We all must become more intentional about sharing the mercy of God with others—the actions and attitudes of which must endure long after the Jubilee Year of Mercy. Mercy must become more the fabric of our lives, parishes, and institutions. We must allow mercy to carry us to new insights, new horizons of service and generosity, new ways of caring for one another, and new ways of being church.

Using Pope Francis' writings, *Becoming a Parish of Mercy* offers a vision of mercy alive in our parishes and provides opportunities for shared reflection and conversation among various parish groups (e.g., clergy, staff, volunteers, and pew-sitters like me). However, before we discuss mercy in the context of parish life, we must first consider the nature of mercy and its role in our own lives. Mercy, at its core, is experienced as love, gift, and liberation, which are at the heart of the gospel message. This book will help you reflect upon these aspects and how you've experienced them as part of your own faith journey. Next, we will shift our focus to mercy in the life of the parish community. Here, mercy takes the shape of accompaniment— the actions and attitudes we adopt that allow us to meet people where they are on their faith journey and gently guide them along the way. Through this book, I hope to accompany you (and your parish) on the journey of faith—and help you encounter, embrace, and share with others the mercy of God, who draws straight with crooked lines, heals, transforms and, ultimately, "triumphs" (Jas 2:13).

Chapter One

Catching the Vision: Mercy as Love, Gift, and Liberation

The Church is commissioned to announce the mercy of God, the beating heart of the Gospel, which in its own way must penetrate the heart and mind of every person. [….] In the present day, as the Church is charged with the task of the new evangelization, the theme of mercy needs to be proposed again and again with new enthusiasm and renewed pastoral action.

It is absolutely essential for the Church and for the credibility of her message that she herself live and testify to mercy. Her language and her gestures must transmit mercy, so as to touch the hearts of all people and inspire them once more to find the road that leads to the Father. (MISERICORDIAE VULTUS, NO. 12)

The Church's first truth is the love of Christ. The Church makes herself a servant of this love and mediates it to all people: a love that forgives and expresses itself in the gift of oneself. Consequently, wherever the Church is present, the mercy of the Father must be evident. In our parishes, communities, associations, and movements, in a word, wherever there are Christians, everyone should find an oasis of mercy.

Vision Statements

A vision statement paints a mental picture of an organization's hopes and dreams. The above quote, taken from *Misericordiae Vultus* (MV)—Pope Francis' official proclamation of the Jubilee Year of Mercy—paints the hope-filled picture of a church focused on forgiveness and accompaniment, meeting people where they are, and existing only to refresh and revive everyone it encounters. At the center of this vision is Christ, "the face of the Father's mercy" (MV, no. 1). Surrounding him are the many faces of believers who joyfully bear his image to others—including you and me! Being a joyful Christian means that our happiness and peace of soul are not to be found in the "self-help" section of the local bookstore; rather, they are found in the service we offer to others. And we do this by meeting people where they are, as they are. This means meeting people's concrete needs and calling them, tenderly, toward a new horizon, a new vision of self, Christ, and the Church. As one saint put it, though I do not recall the name, so I am forced to paraphrase: at the height of spirituality, the only question left is: How can I help you?

Jesus inaugurated the vision of a merciful church (Mt 5:7; Mt 18:21–22; Lk 4:17–19; Tit 3:4–5; 1 Pet 1:3–4) and Francis echoes this vision in his own words: the Church is called to heal, to be an "open door" (EG, no. 46), a people of welcome and understanding, a non-judgmental people, a people *who make room for others*. This includes room to stop or begin, change direction, move forward, to deepen and/or transform; but never room to cower, hide, or disappear. In the Church, there is room for everyone as they are, and not as they should be; because no one is as they should be. That being said, we are all called to greatness: to a greater sharing in (and sharing out) of God's mercy. Francis reminds us that the Church, first and foremost, is a place of healing, an oasis in the many deserts of life.

To keep Francis' vision of a more merciful Church from becoming a mere mirage, we all—especially parishes— must do our part to catch, hold onto, and run with this vision. Indeed, we must begin building parishes of mercy, where mercy is at the center of parish life, flowing outward into every facet in new, life-giving ways:

It [the parish] is a community of communities, a sanctuary where the thirsty come to drink in the midst of their journey, and a center of constant missionary outreach. We must admit, though, that the call to review and renew our parishes has not yet sufficed to bring them nearer to people, to make them environments of living communion and participation, and to make them completely mission-oriented. (EVANGELII GAUDIUM, NO. 28)

Parish life must become more life-giving. And this starts when parishes become more intentional about the giving and receiving of mercy.

Famous Francis

You know you've made it as a pope, popularity-wise, when your visit to the United States (2015) results in your own TV channel complete with 24-hour coverage (Time Warner Cable)—Pope Vision, anyone?—and over an hour of coverage on a popular sports (that's right, sports) radio talk show (*The Dan Patrick Show*, NBC). Francis, or at least the idea of him, is everywhere—an omnipresence that has been labeled by many as the "Francis effect."

Observing Pope Francis' immediate and profound popularity—his provocative comments and inspiring humility, and all the discussion, concern, and hope he has generated—reminds me of watching a rock being dropped into a pond. The rock hits the pond's surface; its splash disrupts the placid water. Soon, however, the water resettles; and although the pond appears to be unchanged, the water level has actually risen, though ever so slightly.

Like the Apostle Peter, Pope Francis is the "rock" (Mt 16:18) who, by his election as pontiff, has been plunged into the deep baptismal waters of the Church, where the thirsty are quenched and sinners are cleansed and renewed. By taking the papal plunge, as it were, and by focusing his papacy on extending the mercy of God to the peripheries, Francis is slowly raising the "water level," so to speak, so that those who at one time felt far from the water's edge may now "drink deeply" (Song 5:1; cf. Pope Francis, Closing Synodal Address, October, 2015).

Through his combination of off-the-cuff, provocative statements—e.g., "Who am I to judge?" (Pope Francis, Interview, en route back to Rome from Rio de Janeiro, July 22, 2013)—and his spontaneous gestures of humility, which have become the stuff of legend, Francis is helping the Church to breach its banks and flow out into new territory: into the hearts of those who are on the margins of faith and society. The water level is rising!

We can't seem to get enough of these Francis feel-good stories. Why? Because deep down, we all know that love, after all, is not meant to be reserved and pooled-up as in a reservoir. Love is to be shared; it must flow into you and me, and from us, out toward others. Love reserved is love spoiled.

Mercy as Love

The Church's first truth is the love of Christ. (MV, NO. 12)

Love is filled with small gestures and words that may appear insignificant; but to the one receiving love, they could very well mean the world. This is so because love, especially Christian-inspired love, is about setting one's self aside and giving to people what they truly need right here, right now (Jas 2:14–17). The Blessed Mother is a great example of this. Catholic tradition views Mary not only as the Mother of God and intercessor par excellence, but also as our spiritual mother; and mothers tend to care about every little detail of their children's lives, no matter how seemingly insignificant. With this in mind, it is no surprise that one of Francis' favorite devotions is to Mary, the Undoer of Knots:

> *But we know one thing: nothing is impossible for God's mercy! Even the most tangled knots are loosened by his grace. And Mary, whose "yes" opened the door for God to undo the knot of the ancient disobedience, is the Mother who patiently and lovingly brings us to God, so that he can untangle the knots of our soul by his fatherly mercy.*
>
> (POPE FRANCIS, OCTOBER 12, 2013)

Let me describe *mercy as love* by telling a story. One day, my five-year-old son (Ben) came into the kitchen where I was busy tying up the trash. He asked me if I wanted to hear a song he had learned. "Of course," I said.

Ben began to sing, "Jesus loves me this I know, for the Bible tells me so…" A classic. After he had finished singing, I asked him if he really knew that Jesus loved him. Nodding his head "yes," I then asked him how he knew. (While my wife and I had read Bible stories to our kids, we didn't do it that often.) Had the Bible really told Ben that Jesus loved him? I wondered. Ben's answer floored me. He said he knew Jesus loved him because his mom and I loved him; and then he said, "And Jesus put you and mom in charge."

Ben's little mind had constructed the following syllogism (i.e., a form of deductive reasoning) with ease: *My parents love me. God put my parents in charge of me. Therefore, God loves me.* I guess I shouldn't have been so surprised by my son's answer. It makes perfect sense. Most children come to know God's love through the love their parents show them. I say "most" because we all know there are far too many children whose belief in God as good and loving is shaken or shattered by a parent's (or parents') lack of love, expressed either through absenteeism, indifference, or even violence.

So, being the teacher that I am, I inquired a little further. I asked Ben *how* he knew that his mom and I loved him. Again his answer was effortless. Rattling off a litany of reasons, he began with the things we give to him (e.g., food, clothing, shelter, and, especially, toys), and ended with, "because you forgive me when I am bad." Ben had connected love with giving and with mercy. In this case, it was *mercy experienced as forgiveness*. After Ben had finished speaking, I smiled at him. He smiled back.

Mercy as Gift

The Church's first truth is the love of Christ. The Church makes herself a servant of this love and mediates it to all people: a love that forgives and expresses itself in the gift of oneself. (MV, NO. 12)

Let's keep the storytelling going. Catechesis, after all, is based on artful storytelling: telling God's story alongside our own— pointing out how the two intertwine and inform each other— and helping other people to do the same.

One day while a student at Franciscan University in Steubenville, Ohio, I was walking in a cemetery and praying my rosary. At the time, I had just left seminary, and I was not sure if I should return or if God had other plans for me. It was a really troubling time in my life. So, with tears running down my cheeks, I asked Mary (she has undone so many knots in my life!) to help me discern her Son's will for me.

I had never been to this cemetery before. It was beautiful and quiet, with lots of walking paths and picturesque rolling hills and ravines. It was the middle of February, and the snow was falling in big heavy flakes. Again, picturesque. The only problem was that I soon became lost. The cemetery is enormous. From where I was, I couldn't see the parking lot. Moreover, with snow blanketing the ground, everything began to look the same. So I took some shelter under a tree. I soon noticed another tree about twenty or so yards away. On the trunk of the tree were something like two blue smudges (I didn't have my glasses at the time).

I walked over to the other tree and saw that those smudges were actually two blue roses—artificial, of course. My Catholic imagination reeled. I began to think that this was a sign from Mary. After all, her favorite color is blue, or so I've been told. I grabbed one of the roses, and immediately there came over me a sense of doubt and anxiety. Like having the proverbial devil and angel appearing on my shoulders and whispering in my ear, I began to doubt that this was a heavenly sign, and I began to think that what I was really doing was taking somebody's flower.

And then, as if it were the angel's turn to speak, I began to calm down. And for the first time I had what I would call an *inner voice* speak to me. This voice was gentle, intimate. I soon believed it to be God's own voice—quite a contrast to the booming voice of God depicted in Cecil B. DeMille's *The Ten Commandments*: "MOSES!!" This quiet voice didn't verbalize anything. It was more like an intuition, an "inspiration," which comes from the Latin "in-spiro" which means "to breathe in" or "inward breath." I was calmed. This inner voice directed me toward a gravestone covered in snow. I brushed the snow off only to find an engraving of St. Thérèse of Lisieux, otherwise known as the Little Flower. There is a tradition that states that if you pray to Thérèse, and your prayer is answered, you will receive a rose. You can imagine my confusion as there I was, holding a rose, yet I had not prayed to Thérèse; I had prayed to Mary.

I continued to walk in no direction in particular. The rose was in my hand. I soon came upon three deer. They raised their heads in my direction and gave me the stare down of my life. They began to walk toward me. I was petrified. (Though I grew up in Iowa, I was not an outdoorsman. I have no outdoors skills whatsoever.) The deer were now standing five feet in front of me. Fearing they would "hoof me"—deer are known for their powerful kicks and punches, aren't they?—I held up my rosary in front of them and said, "This is Our Lady's rosary. She is Queen of Heaven and Earth, and she loves you." Yes, I was talking to the deer. And, no, I didn't have anything to drink earlier. The deer, together, bowed their heads and slowly turned around. I followed them and they led me to the parking lot—to my car, as a matter of fact.

I quickly drove home. My head was reeling: What did all of this mean? Did I really just talk to those deer? I pulled into my driveway and made a beeline for the phone. I called my friend Carolyn and told her everything that had happened. I was stunned by her response and by the fact that she wasn't stunned at all. She told me that she had just finished praying a novena to St. Thérèse for me that day! I couldn't believe it.

But the story doesn't end here. Fast-forward five years. I am standing at the altar in a little parish in Collinsville, Oklahoma, watching my bride walk down the aisle. All of a sudden the memories of my experiences in the cemetery came flooding in, and I realized that the church I was standing in was a shrine to St. Thérèse of Lisieux. More than this, I realized how God, through the intercession of Mary and Thérèse, had guided my discernment, my life, from Steubenville to Collinsville and to the love of my life, Stacy. What a gift!

Again, *mercy is about making room for others.* That day in the cemetery, a door was opened for me; a new path for my life was forged. I didn't deserve it. I am no better than anyone else. I am like Pope Francis, who, in his interview with *America* Magazine (2013), when asked who he was, said, "I am a sinner." God's mercy was experienced as a great gift that day in the cemetery and, again, at the altar. It is mercy that moves God to give gifts to his people.

Mercy as Liberation

Faced with a vision of justice as the mere observance of the law that judges people simply by dividing them into two groups— the just and sinners—Jesus is bent on revealing the great gift of mercy that searches out sinners and offers them pardon and salvation. One can see why, on the basis of such a liberating vision of mercy as a source of new life, Jesus was rejected by the Pharisees and the other teachers of the law. (MV, NO. 20)

One of the most memorable and provocative parables in the gospels is the one popularly referred to as "the prodigal son" (Lk 15:11–32). This parable highlights a few things. First, it highlights the unparalleled generosity of God, whose ways and thoughts are far above our own (Is 55:8). The actions of the father in the parable are not logical; rather, they are motivated by his love for his son and the longing he felt for him. Through the father's actions, I am reminded of the Scripture verse: "Turn to me [my son] and be saved" (cf. Is 45:22). Longing is a powerful motivator. As the Gospel of John notes, it was out of longing (*agapaó*)—a longing for reunion—that God gave to the world his only Son (Jn 3:16).

This parable also indicates that mercy is absolutely a gift. We can't earn it. We don't deserve it. Mercy is free, and it is given to free us. Moreover, the parable offers a sobering reminder of the unintentional division that mercy can cause, especially when the recipient is someone perceived by another to be undeserving; or when the dominant perception is that mercy may only serve to enable someone's misbehavior. There is no doubt that mercy is a messy business that requires much discernment.

Mercy, it seems, is a double-edged sword: it can cut people loose from their bonds, yet perceptions about mercy can also sever the bonds between people. It could well be the case that Jesus was alluding to *mercy itself* when he said to his disciples:

*Do not think that I have come to bring peace on earth; I have
not come to bring peace, but a sword. For I have come to set a
man against his father, and a daughter against her mother,
and a daughter-in-law against her mother-in-law; and a
man's foes will be those of his own household.* (MT 10:34–36)

Jesus speaks these words to his apostles before he sends them
out to proclaim the good news that God's kingdom is near to
all—a kingdom full of mercy:

Finally, this parable highlights a path of accompaniment.
Mercy is not a mere exchange of "I am sorry" and "I forgive
you." This is both a reductionist and legalistic view of mercy—
mercy as transaction, as a trading of goods and services: a *quid
pro quo*. Christian mercy (and I emphasize Christ, here, as he
gives us the example to follow) is an approach; it is a way of
accompanying people. Apology and forgiveness have their
place within the directionality of mercy. Yet, as the parable
demonstrates, mercy does not always wait for an apology.

The path of accompaniment begins with the father *going
out* to meet his son. The father goes out—out of his way, out of
himself—not in anticipation of an apology, which is evidenced
by the father's lack of interest in his son's words, but because
of his longing for his son. In other words, he is already moving
in the direction of mercy. The father then continues to demonstrate his merciful heart by calling for a celebration to be ar-
ranged, as he accompanies his son back home, past the on-
lookers and murmurers. Once at home, the father shows his

mercy a final time by advocating for his younger son, in an attempt to reason with the older son.

Therefore, the path of accompaniment in this parable is first a movement *outward*, followed by an *encounter* (an embrace), and a *return* home, and concluding with a *reception* in the form of food and celebration. Apologies and forgiveness find their places in the experience of *encounter*. Also, the father's pleading with the older son (which was not something befitting a father in the culture of the time) demonstrates a second movement *outward*, in the hope of *encountering* (embracing) the older son and *returning* him to the *reception*. In other words, mercy is an intentional movement toward and alongside another, and not a mere exchange of "I am sorry" for "I forgive you." The path of mercy is marked with actions and attitudes that lead people toward love, gift, and liberation. (More will be said about the key actions and attitudes of mercy in chapter 3.)

Mercy: An Open Door

A Church which "goes forth" is a Church whose doors are open. Going out to others in order to reach the fringes of humanity does not mean rushing out aimlessly into the world. Often it is better simply to slow down, to put aside our eagerness in order to see and listen to others, to stop rushing from one thing to another and to remain with someone who has faltered along the way. At times we have to be like the father of the prodigal son, who always keeps his door open so that when the son

returns, he can readily pass through it. (EG, NO. 46)

God calls us to orient ourselves toward others, making room for them to come to their senses, much like the father did for his prodigal son. This more proactive approach to mercy requires that we yield the power to judge and to "fix" people, and that we not wait for apologies before showing our care and concern. Instead, like the father of the prodigal son, who shows us a path of accompaniment, we must also find ways to *go out* to those who have offended us, *encounter* them, encourage their *return* to us (or to the Church, to God), and be willing to *receive* them in such a way that we keep our doors open—the doors of our hearts and, possibly, the doors of our homes—so that their return to us is not made unnecessarily difficult.

To be sure, being an *open door* is not the same thing as being a *door mat.* Mercy does not call us to sacrifice our own integrity or to suffer unnecessarily the offenses of others. Rather, it is because of our integrity that we *make room* for the possibility that the one (or group) who has offended us will eventually seek to make things right. In the meantime, however, we must continue to show mercy, which means (at minimum) that we pray for those who persecute us (Mt 5:44), and, when appropriate, that we prayerfully discern ways to go out and encounter them as an expression of our Christ-inspired kindness and concern.

Some situations, however, like relationships that are violent and abusive, may demand a permanent separation. Going out to encounter the other may not be the prudent thing to do. However, even in these most unfortunate situations, prayer for the other is still something we are called to do. Through the grace of Christ, no matter how deep the hurt, praying for those who have mistreated us (Lk 6:28) is still possible though it may take time, even a lifetime to get there.

The parable of the prodigal son, and the path of accompaniment it offers, helps to highlight the complexities inherent in the sharing of mercy. Facing the challenge to become more merciful, I draw inspiration from Pope Francis, who notes that such a venture is necessarily a messy business:

> *Here I repeat for the entire Church what I have often said to the priests and laity of Buenos Aires: I prefer a Church which is bruised, hurting and dirty because it has been out on the streets, rather than a Church which is unhealthy from being confined and from clinging to its own security.* (EG, NO. 49)

We must have hearts like open doors in two senses: (1) we must allow ourselves to be accompanied; (2) we must be willing to *go out* and *patiently wait* for others, accompanying them along their journey of faith. We must love the sinner *through* the sin. We are all sinners. And we are all loved by God.

Conclusion

Being merciful means that *we make room for others—room for new opportunities, new blessings, and new life.* Mercy is the core of the gospel message; as such, mercy is the character of the Church's evangelization, and accompaniment is the way we are to evangelize. Pope Francis is offering the Church a vision of mercy expressed as love, gift, and liberation. Together, these point to a more comprehensive (and Christian) understanding of mercy as a path of accompaniment marked by critical phases of encounter, reconciliation, and transformation.

To catch Francis' vision of a more merciful Church we must embrace a more biblical perspective on mercy and wrestle with its intrinsic complexities; and this difficult but rewarding work needs to begin in our individual lives—in our relationships with others and especially in our families, which are referred to so often as "domestic churches" and seen as the cornerstones of parish life.

A postscript: While families are the cornerstones of parish life (and society), we all know people may choose (or the choice is out of their hands) to remain single and/or childless. The single life is a vocation too! Not to mention that many people in our parishes are not ready for marriage (it's not even on their radar), or they have felt the pain of divorce or the loss of a spouse, and so they choose not to marry again. These folks too are essential to parish life. They represent, if you will, the many "stones" stacked in between the family cornerstones, all of which are needed to round out and stabilize a parish community. The fact is, you can't build a parish, much less a parish of mercy, attending only to families—especially only those who come to Mass regularly. A parish of mercy is one that attends to the peripheries, to the marginalized and the anonymous. In a parish of mercy, everyone matters! Are you ready to help build a parish of mercy?

FOR REFLECTION

A Church which "goes forth" is a Church whose doors are open. Going out to others in order to reach the fringes of humanity does not mean rushing out aimlessly into the world. Often it is better simply to slow down, to put aside our eagerness in order to see and listen to others, to stop rushing from one thing to another and to remain with someone who has faltered along the way. At times we have to be like the father of the prodigal son, who always keeps his door open so that when the son returns, he can readily pass through it. (EG, NO. 46)

1] Pope Francis pairs the imagery of "open doors" with the story of the prodigal son to describe the Church's merciful approach to others. Doors are neutral: they can be opened or shut, entrances or exits, locked or unlocked. As you reflect on the many relationships that make up your life, which door (or doors) do you think best describes you? How are you an "open door" for others?

Let me say this once more: God never tires of forgiving us: we are the ones who tire of seeking his mercy. Christ, who told us to forgive one another "seventy times seven" (Mt 18:22) has given us his example: he has forgiven us seventy times seven. Time and time again he bears us on his shoulders. No one can strip us of the dignity bestowed upon us by this boundless and unfailing love. (EG, NO. 3)

2] Here, Francis describes mercy as an example of God's unconditional love. When have you ever experienced a love like this? Do you believe God loves you unconditionally?

The Church which "goes forth" is a community of missionary disciples who take the first step, who are involved and supportive, who bear fruit and rejoice. An evangelizing community knows that the Lord has taken the initiative, he has loved us first (cf. 1 Jn 4:19), and therefore we can move forward, boldly take the initiative, go out to others, seek those who have fallen away, stand [together] at the crossroads and welcome the outcast. Such a community has an endless desire to show mercy, the fruit of its own experience of the power of the Father's infinite mercy. (EG, NO. 24)

3] Is there something keeping you from receiving the love, gift, or liberation you need? Is there something keeping you from being a source of mercy for others? Take the opportunity to name these obstacles and to renounce them in the name of Jesus.

Chapter Two

Evangelization in a New Key: Mercy and the New Evangelization

In the present day, as the Church is charged with the task of the new evangelization, the theme of mercy needs to be proposed again and again with new enthusiasm and renewed pastoral action. It is absolutely essential for the Church and for the credibility of her message that she herself live and testify to mercy. Her language and her gestures must transmit mercy, so

as to touch the hearts of all people and inspire them once more
to find the road that leads to the Father. (MV, NO. 12)

What's "new" about the New Evangelization?

Mercy is "the beating heart of the Gospel" (MV, no. 12). If this is true (and it is!) then everything we do to proclaim the gospel message must begin and end with mercy. In other words, mercy is why we evangelize. It's why we gather as a church. Like those in the gospel stories who have received the mercy of Jesus, we too are called to go out and share God's mercy with others—to share the love, gift, and liberation that mercy has brought to us.

I wrote my doctoral dissertation (2014) on the Church's historical (and developing) understanding and approach to evangelization and catechesis. Part of my dissertation focused on the phenomenon of the New Evangelization by asking the question: "What's new about it?" I began to answer this question by turning to Saint John Paul II's 1983 address to the Latin American Episcopal Conference, in which he called for a "new evangelization," one that was "new in ardor, methods, and expression" (Address to CELAM, March 9, 1983). Reflecting on this statement, I asked myself, "What are these new methods and expressions?" In other words, how do we "do" this new evangelization?

At the time, I thought about the number of ministries that were going on my diocese and in my parish, all of which were aimed, in some way, at conversion (initial and/or ongoing). It was truly amazing, the number of things that were (and still are) happening—services to immigrants, refugees, and the homeless; faith-sharing groups meeting in parishes and in homes; retreats and missions; young adult groups; men's and women's groups; numerous catechetical offerings; inspiring TV and radio ads and more. All of these good works are in line with the New Evangelization's clarion call toward "new ardor, methods, and expression." For example:

- *New ardor:* The above-mentioned opportunities point to our local church's renewed commitment to focus pastoral energies on those who live on the margins of faith and society.

- *New methods:* There is evidence, in these opportunities, of creative and varied ways of proclaiming and witnessing to the gospel message.

- *New expression:* Some of these opportunities were offered bilingually, and others attempted to incorporate technology as a means of fostering a digital discipleship: faith going online.

However, and not to take away anything from the good work that was (and is) happening in my diocese and in dioceses and parishes around the world, it seemed like the response to the New Evangelization was being interpreted as a myriad of

things to do. Something was missing. Indeed, what *was* missing was the shared understanding of the centrality of mercy in
evangelization—that mercy is the heart of the gospel message.
This points us to the notion that mercy is relational, which
means that evangelization is not primarily facilitated by this
or that event or program, no matter how high the quality or
how well it is executed. Evangelization happens between you
and me. *It happens between people.*

Think of parish (or diocesan) programs and events as *moments* of evangelization: snapshots, if you will. But evangelization on the whole is something ongoing and interpersonal. It
has everything to do with extending the mercy of God to others, which requires accompaniment. And as we saw in the parable of the prodigal son, being a merciful person—being an
instrument of mercy in the family, parish, or anywhere else, for
that matter—can cause confusion, frustration, anger, and division. Still, we must try to be merciful in and out of season.

We Walk by Faith...and Together

We are often judged by what we do; so, we often give little attention to who we are or who we might become. Similarly, the
New Evangelization has often been received as a new litany of
programs, events, and opportunities for fostering conversion.
But there is something deeper here. Mercy is the *character* of
the New Evangelization. Saint John Paul II knew this
(*Redemptoris Missio*, no. 44; *Dives in Misericordia*, no. 6), and his
successors have reaffirmed this important truth (Pope Benedict

XVI, Homily on Divine Mercy Sunday, April 15, 2007; Pope Francis, Closing Synodal Address, October 24, 2015). And the *way* of the New Evangelization—how we do it—is through "spiritual accompaniment" (EG, no. 169; *Laudato Si'* [LS], no. 235), which is one of the great gifts Pope Francis offers the Church today. Spiritual accompaniment is what gives the vision of the New Evangelization real traction. It's where the rubber meets the road, if you will. "Spiritual accompaniment" means meeting people—all people—where they are, and forming relationships with them based on trust, respect, and love. And it is by these relationships that we gradually (tenderly) lead people to God. There is a pace to accompaniment, as Francis notes:

> *The pace of this accompaniment must be steady and reassuring, reflecting our closeness and our compassionate gaze which also heals, liberates and encourages growth in the Christian life.* (EG, NO. 169)

We accompany others so that they can experience God's mercy in an incarnate way—in a way that is perceptible to the senses, which includes a physical nearness and a care that involves our mental, spiritual, and bodily energies. We accompany as a way of continuing Christ's own ministry of accompaniment. We accompany others in order to create greater community (and communion) in Christ. We accompany so that others may experience the love, gift, and liberation that come with receiving God's mercy. (More will be said about accompaniment in chapter 3.)

The point here is that when we understand that mercy is the *character* of evangelization, and that accompaniment is the *way* we evangelize, we can begin to see that becoming a church of mercy is, indeed, the goal of the New Evangelization, not a compounding of programs and events *ad infinitum*.

A Sacramental People for Others, not a People for the Sacraments

> *The salvation which God offers us is the work of his mercy....*
> *The Church is sent by Jesus Christ as the sacrament of the*
> *salvation offered by God. Through her evangelizing activity,*
> *she cooperates as an instrument of that divine grace which*
> *works unceasingly and inscrutably.* (EG, no. 112)

I have said a lot so far about evangelization and mercy, but I haven't mentioned the sacraments. The sacramental experience is the privileged way in which Christ accompanies us (I S, no 235). So, where do the sacraments fit into the work of evangelization? This may come as a surprise, but I would suggest that the sacraments not be considered the center (or focus) of Church life. This is not to say that the sacraments are not essential. They are! But rather than occupying the focus of Church life, like a sacred centerpiece of sorts, think of the sacraments as surrounding and penetrating the entire Church. "Church" (*ek-*

klesia), in a Christian sense, means *a people gathered in Christ for each other*. Jesus is the focus of this gathering. But he is not above or apart from his people. In giving up his life for us and calling his Church into being, Jesus, by the Spirit, is within every believer. He abides in those who walk by faith (Jn 14:23; 2 Cor 5:7). So, what does this mean? It means that the center of Church life is not a point but an *ever-widening circle of communion*—which, I think, resonates well with the words of the Second Vatican Council that "the Eucharist is the source and summit of the Christian life" (*Lumen Gentium*, no. 11).

Church is people in relationship to Christ and each other—a people loving and serving together. For their part, the sacraments surround, penetrate, and transform the Church. Therefore, a post-Vatican II view of the sacramental life and its relationship to evangelization could be described not as *preparing a people to live for the sacraments*, but *preparing a sacramental people to live for others*. In a church of mercy, sacraments, while instituted by Christ and administered by him, are not to be thought of as relics or special/graced objects. Sacraments facilitate privileged encounters: encounters with each other and with God.

To explain the interpersonal nature of sacrament a little further—and to demonstrate the creative continuity of Catholic teaching—let me take the definition of "sacrament" from the Baltimore Catechism and connect it with *Lumen Gentium* (LG), the Second Vatican Council's dogmatic teaching on the nature of the Church. The Baltimore Catechism teaches that a sacrament should be thought of as an "outward sign of an inward grace." Isn't that what you and I should be also? Aren't we called to be signs of God's love and mercy in the world? Indeed, we are, which is why the Second Vatican Council teaches that the Church itself reveals God to the world much like a sacrament does (LG, no. 1). The Council goes on to say that the Church's nature can aptly be described as "the People of God" (LG, no. 9). In this light, we can see more clearly that the Church *is Christ in people and people in Christ*—the vine and the branches (Jn 15:5)—who are called to keep "branching out" toward those on the margins of faith and society. And because the Church is a *people in Christ*, it is necessarily *a people for others*. For as "God so loved (longed for) the world that he sent his only son…" (Jn 3:16), the Son, in turn, sends those who believe in him, who are like sacraments, to be outward signs of God's inward love and mercy.

Therefore, mercy (or a parish, which strives to be the collective embodiment of mercy) is people-centered, operating with a shared consciousness by which everyone understands their role as a seeker and finder of others, as reconcilers, and as joyful celebrants of God's great mercy, which is waiting to be shared with everyone. In other words, a church of mercy recognizes that "Jesus is the face of the Father's mercy" (MV, no.1), but refuses to stop at mere recognition, mere understanding. It continues to move forward from recognition to reality in the actualization of the baptismal call each person shares: to be the face of the Father's mercy in the world.

Speaking the Truth in Love and for Love

*The Synod experience also made us better realize that the true
defenders of doctrine are not those who uphold its letter, but its
spirit; not ideas but people; not formulae but the gratuitousness
of God's love and forgiveness. This is in no way to detract from
the importance of formulae—they are necessary—or from the
importance of laws and divine commandments, but rather to
exalt the greatness of the true God, who does not treat us
according to our merits or even according to our works but
solely according to the boundless generosity of his Mercy (cf.
Rom 3:21-30; Ps 129; Lk11:47—54).* (POPE FRANCIS, CLOSING
SYNODAL ADDRESS, OCTOBER 24, 2015)

What about doctrine? Part of evangelizing is sharing Church
teaching with others. So how do we convey the teachings of
the Church in a more merciful way? Let's go back to our description of mercy as *making room for others,* the effects of
which are love, gift, and liberation. And let's ask ourselves the
tough question: Do I share the teaching of the Church with
the intent to help others experience the love, gift, and liberation of God's mercy? Certainly, sharing Church teaching requires discretion and discernment.

Discernment is imperative in catechesis! There is a time
and season for it. This is not a dodge. Even St. Paul appreciated
the role of discernment in the work of preaching and teaching. In his ministry to the Church in Corinth, he notes the

importance of knowing those to whom you minister (and we are all called to minister in different ways), and where they are on their journey *to* or *of* faith (1 Cor 3:1–9).

One consideration to keep in mind is whether or not a person has received the gift of faith. Faith, like a tree, is known by its fruits (Lk 6:44). Typically, a person's lack of belief in Jesus as the Christ, the Son of God, is due to a lack of personal encounter with him, which is why St. John Paul II emphatically states that "the definitive aim of catechesis is to put people not only in touch but in communion, in intimacy, with Jesus Christ" (*Catechesi Tradendae*, no. 5). Frankly, for a person who has not received the gift of faith, catechesis does little good, because its very intent is to expound on the *mysteries of faith*. In other words, faith is a point of departure for catechesis. Without it, what we might call "catechesis" is merely a philosophizing of sorts—a way to demonstrate the reasonableness of faith. This activity, which is often called apologetics, is a good thing. But it is no substitute for catechesis. Reason can prepare people for faith, but the two are not synonymous. Therefore, in such a situation where faith has not been received, evangelizing by appealing to doctrine may be ineffective, even inappropriate—much like putting the cart before the horse.

Using Jesus' words concerning the Sabbath (Mk 2:27) as an analogy, we can say that humankind is not at the service of Catholic doctrine; rather, Catholic doctrine is at the service of humankind.

Catechesis too must follow the path of spiritual accompa-

niment, which begins where people are: their concrete situation, along with all that has informed (and misinformed) their
views of self, others, and God. Therefore, Francis writes:

> *Preachers often use words learned during their studies and in*
> *specialized settings which are not part of the ordinary*
> *language of their hearers. These are words that are suitable in*
> *theology or catechesis, but whose meaning is incomprehensible*
> *to the majority of Christians. The greatest risk for a preacher is*
> *that he becomes so accustomed to his own language that he*
> *thinks that everyone else naturally understands and uses it. If*
> *we wish to adapt to people's language and to reach them with*
> *God's word, we need to share in their lives and pay loving*
> *attention to them.* (EG, NO. 158)

Let me ask you a question: While it is true that *instructing the ig-*
norant is considered a *spiritual work of mercy*, is this where we
ought to begin our accompaniment, especially if we do not have
a relationship with the person and, therefore, have not yet estab-
lished any credibility as someone who is knowledgeable in matters of faith or, more importantly, as someone who is worthy of
trust, respect, or love? As Mark notes throughout his gospel, even
the demons knew well who Jesus was! But unlike the demons,
we never want to present the truth of the gospel message as a
means of reproach, accusation, or exclusion, which, at times, may
be our secret motivation or may be perceived as such by one to
whom we are unknown, unverified. So much catechesis happens

impersonally—outside of the bonds of trust and love. This cannot be the standard operating procedure for catechesis in a parish of mercy.

As stated earlier, catechesis must follow the pace of accompaniment. In the following quote, Pope Francis offers the catechist a starting point for any and all situations of accompaniment. This starting point is also a point of return which, he says, "must ring out over and over":

> On the lips of the catechist the first proclamation must ring out over and over: "Jesus Christ loves you; he gave his life to save you; and now he is living at your side every day to enlighten, strengthen and free you." This first proclamation is called "first" not because it exists at the beginning and can then be forgotten or replaced by other more important things. It is first in a qualitative sense because it is the principal proclamation, the one which we must hear again and again in different ways, the one which we must announce one way or another throughout the process of catechesis, at every level and moment. (EG, NO. 164)

Relationships: the Bedrock of Evangelization

> The individualism of our postmodern and globalized era favors a lifestyle which weakens the development and stability of personal relationships and distorts family bonds. Pastoral activity needs to bring out more clearly the fact that our

relationship with the Father demands and encourages a
communion which heals, promotes and reinforces
interpersonal bonds. (EG, NO. 67)

Mercy is the character of the New Evangelization, and accompaniment is the way. A *church* signifies an ever-expanding network of sacramentalized people, called to extend the mercy of God to all those they meet. This network is made up of relationships—some weak and some strong, some healthy and some not—a church is not a perfect society! The goal, however, is that by God's grace and our cooperation, these relational bonds will eventually be characterized by three things: *respect, trust,* and *love.* Sherry Weddell's book *Forming Intentional Disciples* (2012) outlines the importance of interpersonal relationships as essential to religious conversion and discipleship. People are relational. God made us this way. Should it be any surprise, then, that any effort to evangelize must first be rooted in cultivating positive relationships?

Why must we seek to cultivate relationships rooted in *respect, trust,* and *love?* Unfortunately, the focus of this book does not permit me to explore this question more in depth. However, I will say that, together, these words have to do with a person's credibility, which, in a Christian sense, can be described as a person's *perceived ability* to receive the woundedness of others and nurture it in a Christlike way—the way of mercy—which leads to love, gift, and liberation in Jesus' name. In 1975, Pope Paul VI wrote an exhortation titled *Evangelii*

Nuntiandi. In it he shared his thoughts on how the Church might evangelize in an increasingly modern (i.e., secularized) world. At one point, he states that people today listen more to witnesses than they do to teachers (EN, nos. 41, 76). Witness, we can say, is the animating principle (the soul) of accompaniment and, therefore, of mercy. Witness is the way we signal to others that we are open to sharing our faith; and, I might add, this does not mean beating people over the head with it! The pace of accompaniment should always be gentle, tender, and gradual.

Paul VI also reminds us that the entire Church, both on the corporate level and the level of the individual person, is called to bear witness to the world. But before it does this, the Church itself must be evangelized (EN, no. 15); that is, the faithful need to recognize and own their identity as disciples— as people who are called by God to witness to their faith 24/7. This does not mean standing on street corners and "thumping" our Bibles. It does, however, mean intentionally considering how we might express our faith in little ways each day, in our homes, at work, in the parish, and in the wider community. When it comes to evangelization, our witness is everything; therefore, it must be credible.

A Sourpuss Does Not a Disciple Make

*One of the more serious temptations which stifle boldness and
zeal is a defeatism which turns us into querulous and*

disillusioned pessimists, "sourpusses."...If we start without
confidence, we have already lost half the battle and we bury
our talents. While painfully aware of our own frailties, we
have to march on without giving in, keeping in mind what the
Lord said to Saint Paul: "My grace is sufficient for you, for my
power is made perfect in weakness" (2 Cor 12:9). Christian
triumph is always a cross, yet a cross which is at the same time
a victorious banner borne with aggressive tenderness against
the assaults of evil. The evil spirit of defeatism is brother to the
temptation to separate, before its time, the wheat from the
weeds; it is the fruit of an anxious and self-centered lack of
trust. (EG, NO. 85)

Credibility is key. Let me share a quick story about the effect a
non-credible witness had on my seven-year-old son, Mikey,
which is a reminder that we are witnesses 24/7. Our family was
at Mass and the congregation began to sing the Alleluia before
the proclamation of the Gospel. The choir provided some rous-
ing music—complete with voices, tambourines, and guitars,
which in my Catholic experience constitutes "the works"! The
people around us were doing their best to sing God's praises.
Looking around, Mikey tugged on my sleeve and motioned for
me to stoop down to hear him. He said, "Daddy, the music is so
happy but everyone looks so sad. What's wrong with them?" I
looked around and saw what he was seeing. The congregation
was singing God's praises, but their bodies and faces were
speaking another language. People's faces looked tired, and it

wasn't even the early Mass! Some folks were hunched over looking at the ground. Others were looking at their watches or phones. Seeing this, I didn't know what to tell Mikey other than "Not everyone likes to sing…people are praying in their own way."

While this may be true, I knew it wasn't the full truth. Mass is not a performance, but it is also not perfunctory. People did appear to be "going through the motions." Then Mikey interrupted my thoughts and said to me, "Daddy, I learned in school that if you are happy and you know it, then your face will surely show it. These people don't look happy." He was right. In that brief exchange with my son, I was reminded that the baptized are called to be witnesses to their faith 24/7—always ready to share with others the hope they have inside them and the reason for it (1 Pet 3:15). Maybe some of the people at that Mass had no reason to be there other than that's what Catholics are supposed to do or because they are afraid of what might happen (eternally) if they don't.

Now, of course, I am not suggesting that we need to be happy all of the time. That's not realistic. But I am saying that evangelization and, therefore, becoming a parish of mercy begins with individual people (and eventually the entire parish community) becoming aware of (and committed to) their role of witness. And this witness must be credible. If we say to others that we are happy to be Catholic but then are seen singing Alleluias like they were funeral dirges, others may have a right to question our credibility. I will say more about the attitude of *joy* in the next chapter, as part of the key actions and attitudes Pope Francis gives us for becoming a parish of mercy. For now, Francis' own words on the matter will suffice:

> *Joy, which is like the sign of a Christian. A Christian without joy is either not a Christian or he is sick. There's no other type! He is not doing well health-wise! A healthy Christian is a joyful Christian.* (HOMILY, MAY 21, 2014)

Conclusion

Mercy is "the beating heart of the Gospel" (MV, no. 12); therefore, mercy must also be fundamental to the Church's mission of evangelization, especially the New Evangelization, which seeks to propose the gospel in today's world with "new ardor, methods, and expression." To give the New Evangelization greater traction going forward, we must identify its character and way. The character of the New Evangelization is *mercy,* and the way is *spiritual accompaniment.* Evangelization takes place between people: it is fundamentally relational. The Church is a network of sacramentalized people who share Christ through and with each other and, ultimately, with the world. A church of mercy puts people first in every facet of its life.

To evangelize more effectively, we must first learn how to cultivate relationships based on *respect, trust,* and *love.* Such qualities speak to the credibility of our witness, which is more vital than ever today. All are called to be witnesses 24/7. We all need to become more aware of this call and then pray for a desire to respond to it more often, especially when sharing our witness seems awkward or difficult. We need not always witness with words. Sometimes, actions speak louder and more convincingly.

The following chapter will discuss the key actions and attitudes of spiritual accompaniment that Pope Francis offers the Church today. It will also discuss the role of witness as essential to fostering religious conversion in others and in our own hearts, according to the phases of spiritual accompaniment. If your parish seems too quiet, too still for your taste right now, just remember that after the tomb came the resurrection. Are you ready to help your parish rise up? Are you ready to help your fellow clergy, staff, and fellow parishioners awaken to the call to accompaniment? If so, read on.

FOR REFLECTION

*This insidious worldliness is evident in a number of attitudes
which appear opposed, yet all have the same pretense of
"taking over the space of the Church." In some people we see
an ostentatious preoccupation for the liturgy, for doctrine and
for the Church's prestige, but without any concern that the
Gospel have a real impact on God's faithful people and the
concrete needs of the present time.* (EG, NO. 95)

1] Becoming a more merciful parish is about putting people
first in all facets of parish life. In what ways are you (your parish) already doing this? Can you identify attitudes or actions
occurring within your parish that appear to be putting people
and their real needs last? Another way to measure your parish's impact on its parishioners is to ask yourself the question:
If our parish didn't exist, who would notice?

---

*The individualism of our postmodern and globalized era
favors a lifestyle which weakens the development and stability
of personal relationships and distorts family bonds. Pastoral
activity needs to bring out more clearly the fact that our
relationship with the Father demands and encourages a
communion which heals, promotes and reinforces
interpersonal bonds.* (EG, NO. 67)

2] Relationships based on respect, trust, and love form the bedrock of evangelization. In fact, most sociologists of religion agree that people choose to convert to new faiths and religions based on the belief that the relationships they will experience will be more meaningful and life-giving than their current relationships. How does your parish help people connect with each other in meaningful ways? Do you think of your parish as a hub of connectedness? Why or why not?

At times how hard it seems to forgive! And yet pardon is the instrument placed into our fragile hands to attain serenity of heart. To let go of anger, wrath, violence, and revenge are necessary conditions to living joyfully. (MV, NO. 9)

3] For the Christian, joy is the fruit of reconciliation. How could your parish provide opportunities for people, both sacramentally and non-sacramentally, to experience the joy of reconciliation? How could your parish encourage reconciliation in people's homes and workplaces?

Chapter Three

Opening Your Parish Doors: The "Key" Actions and Attitudes of Accompaniment

The Church is called to be the house of the Father, with doors always wide open. One concrete sign of such openness is that our church doors should always be open, so that if someone,

moved by the Spirit, comes there looking for God, he or she
will not find a closed door. (EG, NO. 47)

It's review time. So far I've talked a lot about mercy itself—mercy as making room for others; mercy as love, gift, and liberation; and mercy as the heart of the gospel message. What is clear from this is that whatever we do to share the gospel message (i.e., evangelization) must begin and end with mercy. I also mentioned that mercy is the *character* of the New Evangelization, and spiritual accompaniment is the *way*. This chapter is all about how we "do" mercy, which is to say: how we ourselves (our parish) can accompany people more intentionally.

Disciples accompany. They *go out* into the world, *invite* others into a community of faith, and *send* them out into the world renewed and ready for mission. Disciples themselves are the real open doors of a merciful parish. These doors are mobile, not stationary; they are entrances, never exits. The journey of accompaniment begins and ends through open doors such as these.

Open Sesame! Becoming an Open Door

The quote at the beginning of this chapter speaks about the Church as an open door. The Church, again, is the People of God. So, in a sense, the quote asks the question: As a person of God, what kind of door are you? To put it another way: How are you like an open door when it comes to your faith? Is there anything about the Catholic faith itself, or about sharing the faith, that prompts you to become a closed door?

Doors are neutral. They can be open, shut, locked or unlocked, exits or entrances. Doors can be revolving too. While giving a presentation on becoming a church of mercy, I asked a lady what kind of a door she was, and she described herself as a "trap door." She said she liked to debate the Catholic faith with people of other faith traditions and then "catch" them saying something she "knows" or "feels" to be untrue. I looked at her and thought, "'Come in! Come in!' said the spider to the fly."

Besides being a trap door, this woman was also an "exit," in the sense that she was someone whose words and actions could easily drive people away from the Church, or even from faith in Christ. A parish of mercy cannot be filled with such "exit signs." Rather, it must focus on creating a culture of openness, calling every individual and family to take their role as witness and companion seriously. Catholics who tend to be more of a "trap door" or an "exit" cannot (or will not) accept (or maybe they do not understand) that they are called, as are all the baptized faithful, to be, like Jesus, the face of the Father's mercy to others.

To be sure, being an "open door" does not mean being a "door mat." Being open to God, to others, and to the changing circumstances of life does not mean we give up our sense of self or our dignity. Sometimes, our doors need to be closed to others, as is the case when we need some alone time or some time away to gain a better perspective on things. Even Jesus needed some time to himself (Lk 5:16)! We also need to close our doors when relationships become abusive or violent. In such cases, it is the responsibility of others (e.g., a pastor, counselor, relative, friend) to open their doors and intervene. However, outside of these exceptional situations, we need to try to be more of an open door in our everyday lives. By doing this, we have a better chance of being, like Jesus, the face of the Father's mercy for others.

So what does it mean to be an open door? In a general sense, we can say that people who are open doors are those who are actively seeking to establish or deepen relationships with others around them in ways that make Christ's mercy more visible, more tangible. More specifically, an open door is someone who is a *daily discerner*—one who is open to receiving God's direction and guidance each day. This includes, of course, being open to the surprises God may have in store for us. Such surprises may come to us gift-wrapped as blessings or challenges. It is my experience that most challenges are actually blessings in disguise. Being an open door also means being a *cross bearer*—someone who is open to sharing another's burdens. This means being a person of forgiveness and hope for others—a Simon of Cyrene to those around you who are bearing their crosses.

Let me give you a personal example of being an open door. I was rolling into the church parking lot at 4:59 pm, trying to make the 5:00 pm Saturday evening Mass. I sneaked into the back pew. (This was before I was married with children: it's impossible to "sneak" anywhere with a family in tow!) I noticed that the woman in front of me kept blowing her nose. She was quickly going through her tissues. I also noticed that she would put her hands up to her face every so often. It became obvious that she was crying.

As the Mass continued, I focused more on this woman and what she might be going through. I wondered if I should do something for her. But what could I do? I thought about talking to her after Mass, asking her if she was okay (of course, she wasn't). I thought about praying for her. That was easy enough—far less commitment required and little chance of awkwardness or embarrassment. Prayer should never be a way to avoid meeting the real needs of others (Jas 2:15–16). This woman didn't need prayer. She needed a hand.

I was inspired to reach out to this woman and put my hand on her shoulder. I had no idea how she would react. If she was like my mother, whom I love dearly, such a gesture would have surprised her, causing her to jerk away violently. Despite this possibility, I took the risk, reached out my hand, and touched her shoulder. The woman didn't move a muscle. She didn't even look to see who was touching her. She only reached back and grabbed my hand firmly. It felt like she was holding on for dear life. Maybe she had been praying for a hand to hold.

After a few minutes, she let go of my hand. Mass concluded, and we began to file out the doors. I walked next to her, but we didn't exchange any words. The woman only looked at me and mouthed the words "thank you." Remember: mercy is about making room for others, room for new life, new blessing and opportunity. This woman needed a door opened for her so she could enter into a new experience of life—an experience of care and consolation. For a moment, I was that door. Mine was the face of the Father's mercy.

A Particular Face of Mercy

> *On a day like any other, as Matthew, the tax collector, was seated at his table, Jesus passed by, saw him, came up to him and said: "Follow me." Matthew got up and followed him. Jesus looked at him. How strong was the love in that look of Jesus, which moved Matthew to do what he did! What power must have been in his eyes to make Matthew get up from his table! [...] Jesus stopped; he did not quickly turn away. He looked at Matthew calmly, peacefully. He looked at him with eyes of mercy; he looked at him as no one had ever looked at him before. And that look unlocked Matthew's heart; it set him free, it healed him, it gave him hope, a new life, as it did to Zacchaeus, to Bartimaeus, to Mary Magdalen, to Peter, and to each of us.* (POPE FRANCIS, HOMILY, SEPTEMBER 21, 2015)

One day, I took a tour of the Basilica of the National Shrine of the Immaculate Conception in Washington, DC. What a glorious building! The tour guide suggested that I begin the tour by standing at the front doors of the nave (the main part of the church) and walk up the center aisle, while keeping my focus on the face of Jesus—part of the enormous mosaic known as Christ in Majesty, situated in the north apse.

Let me describe the mosaic to you. Facing it, you see Jesus raised from the dead and seated in judgment. His body is ripped with muscles (he must have been working out in the underworld), and part of his torso is cloaked in a red robe. His arms are held in a "touchdown" posture. Fire is shooting out from his head at three different points, and his right brow is furrowed—pretty intimidating, if you ask me. Okay, it's downright frightening. This image of Jesus embodies the famous line from the movie *The Terminator*: "I'll be back."

So, I began to walk down the center aisle, keeping my eyes on the face of Jesus, who is ready to judge the world. As I moved closer to the mosaic, I noticed that part of Jesus' face appeared gentle, even serene. His left eye looked rounder than the right, the brow not as furrowed. When I was standing underneath the image, Jesus' face appeared merciful. At that point, the tour guide told me that the mosaic was designed to depict both the justice and mercy of God, which is why one side of the face appears "angrier" than the other.

I appreciated the juxtaposition. But I also noticed that it was difficult to see the merciful features of Jesus' face from far away. And this led me to appreciate something much deeper: that people who feel (or think they are) far from Jesus, tend to view him as angry and full of judgment—as a "trap door," if you will, just waiting to say "gotcha!" On the other hand, those who have drawn close enough to Christ and personally experienced God's mercy cannot help but see "the face of the Father's mercy" (MV, no. 1). I wonder: How does Jesus look at you?

Dynamics of Religious Conversion

We need to give our hearts to our companions along the way, without suspicion or distrust.…When we give of ourselves, we discover our true identity as children of God in the image of the Father and, like him, givers of life; we discover that we are brothers and sisters of Jesus, to whom we bear witness. This is what it means to evangelize; this is the new revolution—for our faith is always revolutionary—this is our deepest and most enduring cry. (POPE FRANCIS, HOMILY, JULY 7, 2015)

Most sociologists of religion agree that people typically convert to a religion or to another community of faith or tradition for a single reason: meaningful relationships. Ritual, doctrine, sacred traditions, and devotions all have their place in the life of faith. But when it comes to conversion, people tend to convert because they believe that the relationships they will make in this new faith community or religion will be more meaningful than their current relationships (see Rodney Stark, *Rise of Christianity*, 1997). Therefore, parishes that evangelize effectively are *communities engaged in the work of engagement*: getting to know people and building relationships based on trust, respect, and love. Parish programs, events, and initiatives are im-

portant. However, solid relationships form the bedrock of evangelization.

I am a visual learner. The graph below shows an X- and
Y-axis and a plotted line indicating growth (depth) of conversion. (And, no, I don't think conversion is ever this linear; I
will address that shortly.) Looking at the graph: the Y-axis indicates our efforts to evangelize. These may include parish programs and events (i.e., corporate efforts) or personal efforts
such as the many actions and moments that make up our own
public witness of faith. The X-axis denotes the depth of the
relationship formed between the evangelizer and the one being evangelized. But how does one measure the depth of a relationship? By the degree of trust, respect, and love that is felt,
shared, and acknowledged by those involved.

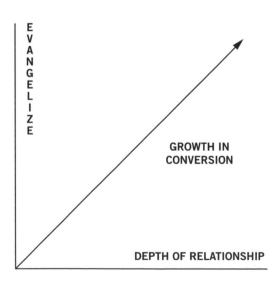

What this graph reveals is that the higher up the Y-axis we go; that is, the more sophisticated or intense the effort to evangelize, the deeper the relationship must become. For example, opening a door for a person or smiling at someone requires little to no interpersonal commitment. We (hopefully) do these kinds of things all the time and for total strangers. We might label these actions as *random acts of kindness*. Many of the corporal and spiritual works of mercy could be labeled as such (e.g., pray for the living and the dead, bear wrongs patiently, give food and drink to the hungry and thirsty, clothe the naked, etc.). This is not to say that such works are unimportant. They are very important! I am only making the distinction between such actions and efforts to evangelize, which take a greater level of interpersonal commitment.

Relationships take time. There is no getting around this. I tell myself this all the time. I know that when it comes to evangelization I am only planting seeds. However, if I am honest with myself, I want to think that I am planting full-grown trees—which, of course, is not true. Evangelization is rooted in relationships; therefore, it takes time. If your idea of evangelization is simply to pray for someone's conversion (and do it privately), hand someone a Bible, or rattle off paragraphs of the Catechism to someone you don't know (or don't know well), you are not doing the work of accompaniment. Accompaniment moves at the pace of the relationship being forged between the evangelizer and the one being evangelized. Of course, all authentic evangelization is the initiative of the Sprit. And where grace is involved/invited, the conversion timeline may speed up, though it may also slow down. In addition, it is important to note that the one evangelizing is also formed by the relationship he or she enters into. As a lay minister, I can't tell you how many times people have formed/inspired/transformed me by their own response to God's grace.

Because evangelization is built on relationships, it is paramount that the evangelizer's credibility be confirmed: that he or she talks and "walks" the faith. Confirmation is achieved by the intentionality and consistency with which we conduct ourselves and relate to others on a daily basis. This means that our deeds must reflect our words, and that we exhibit no duplicity in our private and public personae. Authenticity and transparency are the most critical ingredients of a powerful witness of faith.

Key Actions and Attitudes
of Spiritual Accompaniment

Love, after all, can never be just an abstraction. By its very nature, it indicates something concrete: intentions, attitudes, and behaviors that are shown in daily living. The mercy of God is his loving concern for each one of us. He feels responsible; that is, he desires our well-being and he wants to see us happy, full of joy, and peaceful. This is the path which the merciful love of Christians must also travel. As the Father loves, so do his children. Just as he is merciful, so we are called to be merciful to each other. (MV, NO. 9)

We evangelize by accompanying others. Pope Francis has given the Church key actions and attitudes of accompaniment. These actions and attitudes appear in Francis' writings and speeches, homilies and addresses, on the themes of mercy and evangelization (mission). What follows is not an official list, but more of a living compendium. Let's start with the actions of accompaniment. As you can see on the following pages, what we are talking about isn't rocket science, nor are these actions particularly Catholic or religious in nature. In fact, they are quite *secular*. I use this term specifically, here, to note its more unfamiliar usage. Secular can mean something long term or of an indefinite duration. This, I think, is the perfect word to describe accompaniment; because when we begin to accompany, we don't know how long the journey will last, what it will be like, or where it will go.

Actions of Accompaniment

- Go out
- Invite/Welcome
- Listen
- Serve
- Pray (with)
- Heal/Forgive
- Empower/encourage
- Worship (with)
- Bless
- Verbally Teach/Preach

Go out

Yet the drive to go forth and give, to go out from ourselves, to keep pressing forward in our sowing of the good seed, remains ever present. The Lord says: "Let us go on to the next towns that I may preach there also, for that is why I came out" (Mk 1:38). Once the seed has been sown in one place, Jesus does not stay behind to explain things or to perform more signs; the Spirit moves him to go forth to other towns. (EG, NO. 21)

Going out can describe something directional, like "going somewhere." It can also mean going out of yourself, which may include going out of your comfort zone, your routine, your perceptions of self and God, and/or your worldview. *Going out* has to do with opening a door (there's that phrase again!)—it is an opening up to the new. By going out, you are making new room for yourself so that you can make room for others.

Let me give you an example that is also tied to the accompaniment action of forgiveness. I know a woman whose husband cheated with her best friend. The couple eventually divorced. However, the two (former) friends attended the same church. Sunday after Sunday they saw each other in the pews (this went on for years!), but neither spoke to the other. One day, after Mass, I watched in surprise as the divorcée approached her former friend and forgave her. The two women cried on each other's shoulders. It was an incredible scene.

After they parted ways, I asked the divorcée what made her decide to forgive. She told me that she did it for two reasons. First, she had to let go of the anger and resentment that had been eating away at her all these years. Second, she would want to be forgiven if she had been "the other woman." What an example of the gospel in action! This woman made room in her heart for forgiveness; and, in turn, she made room for her friend, setting her free from the guilt which she had been carrying around for years.

Invite/Welcome

> *Someone good at such accompaniment does not give in to*
> *frustrations or fears. He or she invites others to let themselves*
> *be healed, to take up their mat, embrace the cross, leave all*
> *behind and go forth ever anew to proclaim the Gospel.*
> (EG, NO. 172)

> *The Church must be a place of mercy freely given, where*
> *everyone can feel welcomed, loved, forgiven and encouraged to*
> *live the good life of the Gospel.* (EG, NO. 114)

Invite/welcome: these are two of the most overlooked qualities of discipleship. Jesus invited himself to people's homes (Zacchaeus); his disciples brought people to him to be healed, fed, and forgiven. Many times Jesus invited people to stay with him. At the first Pentecost after Jesus' resurrection, we see the disciples continuing the work of invitation—inviting people from all over to be baptized. The first disciples were engaged in the work of invitation: they were opening doors for others and inviting them to walk through, to receive new life and blessing. We could learn a lot from them.

Likewise, welcoming others has everything to do with opening the door for people, literally, and letting them know that you are happy to see them, that they are important, that it is good for them to be here! I know parishes often task committees or groups with welcoming people to Mass, but I caution against this practice. It's a double-edged sword. Once a group has been signaled as "the welcoming committee," or as the group that contacts parishioners and invites them to parish events, then the congregation as a whole no longer feels responsible for such things. The truth is that we need committees *and* we need individuals inviting and welcoming others to church.

Listen

> In order to be capable of mercy, therefore, we must first of all dispose ourselves to listen to the Word of God. This means rediscovering the value of silence in order to meditate on the Word that comes to us. In this way, it will be possible to contemplate God's mercy and adopt it as our lifestyle.
>
> (MV, NO. 13)

When faced with evil deeds, even in the face of serious crimes,
it is the time to listen to the cry of innocent people who are
deprived of their property, their dignity, their feelings, and
even their very lives. (MV, NO. 19)

As Christians, we are called to listen and to watch for God's actions in the world. We listen to the word of God: the Scriptures. And we listen to the Word of God: Jesus, who calls us to hear the cry of the poor. There are many kinds of poverty: material, emotional, spiritual, moral, relational, etc. We are called to accompany others by opening our ears to hear them— their needs and concerns, as well as their hopes and joys.

Serve

This loving attentiveness is the beginning of a true concern for
their person which inspires me effectively to seek their good.
This entails appreciating the poor in their goodness, in their
experience of life, in their culture, and in their ways of living
the faith. True love is always contemplative, and permits us to
serve the other not out of necessity or vanity, but rather
because he or she is beautiful above and beyond mere
appearances.... (EG, NO. 199)

I aspire to be a deacon. My wife and I are in formation for the permanent diaconate. We are constantly reminded that *deacon* means *servant*. "Service," after all, is the meaning of the New

Testament Greek word *diakonia*. However, it would be misleading to think that service is only the work of the ordained. As is the case with each of these actions of accompaniment, everyone is called to the work of service. Serving doesn't have to be scheduled or organized. It can be informal and spontaneous.

For example, I remember being in Mass (my family was sitting in the gathering space), and a woman walked into the gathering space and fell to her knees. She was exhausted. I immediately got up and assisted her. It turned out that she had not eaten in a long time, and her blood sugar was low. When I got back to my seat, after giving her some juice and a cookie, I said to my wife, "I feel so deacon-like." She responded, "You were disciple-like." She was right! Disciples are people who keep their doors open, always on the lookout for others and ready to help them.

The Pace of Accompaniment

> *The pace of this accompaniment must be steady and reassuring, reflecting our closeness and our compassionate gaze which also heals, liberates and encourages growth in the Christian life.* (EG, NO. 169)

The Scriptures reveal God as the Great Companion; that is, God deliberately reveals himself gradually, progressively, to his creation. From the story of Adam and Eve in the Garden to the post-resurrection evangelization of the Gentiles, the pages of Scripture are filled with stories of God accompanying people. These stories usually begin with an encounter between a person (or a group of people) and God. As the relationship develops over time, an experience of faith is fostered, especially when God continues to make good on his promises despite the person's or people's inability to keep faith. At some point during the accompaniment process, and guided by inspiration, God's people come to articulate their beliefs and evaluate their relationship with God. In doing so, they pass on to the next generation certain laws, guidelines, teachings, prayers, and rituals that will foster in them an authentic understanding and response of faith.

God's accompaniment of people has been going on for millennia, which tells us that God certainly takes his time when it comes to revealing who he is and what his plan is for his people. The truth is, we are still waiting for the fullness of God's plan to come to fruition: the consummation of the world and the reconciliation, in Christ, of a groaning creation (Rom 8:18–21). While we ourselves don't have millennia's worth of time to accompany others—though there is something to be said about saintly intercession!—we see that there is a pace to accompaniment, a process. Like God, we gradually open ourselves, our experiences and beliefs, to others. We don't start with *what we believe*, but with *who we are* and *in whom we believe*. When we share ourselves with others, and we share with them our relationship with God—then we have the opportunity to share what we believe about God and why we believe it. Always put people before propositions.

In order to see this—again, visuals help—I have grouped the actions of accompaniment into three phases: (1) encounter, (2) sharing faith experiences, and (3) articulating faith.

ACTIONS		
Go out		
Invite		
Welcome anew	encountering others	1
Listen		
Serve		
Pray (with)		
Heal		
Empower	sharing faith experiences	2
Worship (with)		
Bless		
Verbally teach/preach	articulating faith	3

Although there is an obvious ordering here, these actions are fluid and, therefore, often repeated. So, one could argue—and one may be right—that the action of *blessing* or *prayer* belongs to the phase of *encounter*. Similarly, some may begin their accompaniment by articulating faith (teaching and verbal preaching) rather than through an experience of encounter. While anything is possible with God, my experience of accompanying others (and being accompanied) tells me that the above ordering gives a person the best chance to accompany a person for the long haul. Now, let's put these phases on our conversion graph:

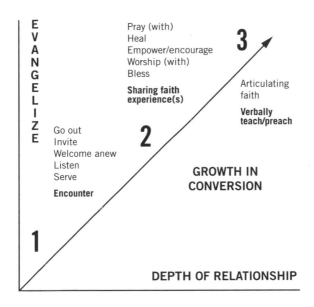

The actions of encounter precipitate and prepare for the sharing of faith experiences which, in turn, helps to shape our understanding of the *content* of faith (i.e., what we believe as Catholics). Our experience of faith is an important key for interpreting what we believe. Information without formation is like being "in the know" without having *known* what it is like to be "in"; that is, to be in relationship with Jesus and his body, the Church. To be a disciple is to be aware of, committed to, and guided by one's relationship with God. It is very possible to be informed about the faith but not be a disciple. But one cannot be a disciple without having been formed by faith. The disciple brings together, in himself or herself, both the knowledge and the experience of faith, which gives shape (and credibility) to his or her personal witness of faith.

Let's get back to God, our Great Companion. God doesn't begin accompanying by pronouncing laws or doctrines (Articulating Faith), but by introducing himself (Encounter) and establishing, time and again, through blessing and miracle (Sharing Faith Experience), the credibility of his divine identity: that he is our merciful Father. Want proof? Take the example of God and Moses: God meets Moses in the burning bush and introduces himself by sharing with Moses his sacred name (Encounter). Then, God accompanies Moses through a series of signs and wonders, as Moses tries to liberate God's people from slavery (Sharing Faith Experience). Finally, after God has demonstrated his credibility and earned Moses' trust, he shares his commandments with him (Articulate Faith). Each phase of accompaniment provides for a new experience of mercy and an opportunity for deeper conversion.

Having the Right Attitude

Remember when I said earlier that religious conversion is not a nice, linear line? For most people, including myself, it is more like taking two steps up, one down; many steps meandering in one direction and then in another; crossing back and forth many times while slowly moving upward.

Everyone can agree that life includes ups and downs. Our

faith, which is an incarnate faith, is not immune to change or circumstance. Bodily, psychic, and relational changes can affect, for better or worse, our perceptions of God and our trust in God—his existence, his goodness, and our own as well. As the theological adage goes: *faith builds on nature*.

Taking one step forward and two steps back is an experience that many people can identify with. This truth, applied to the journey of faith, is why the *Catechism of the Catholic Church* (CCC) notes that the Christian life is marked by the need for both penance and renewal:

> *Christ's call to conversion continues to resound in the lives of Christians. This second conversion is an uninterrupted task for the whole Church who, "clasping sinners to her bosom, [is] at once holy and always in need of purification, [and] follows constantly the path of penance and renewal.* (CCC, NO. 1428)

The above quote even refers to a "second conversion," which speaks to our need to deepen the initial conversion begun at baptism. However, I would take this quote even further by saying that some of us even need a third, fourth, fifth, etc., conversion. I have yet to meet a Christian who said their conversion experience has been nothing but onward and upward from the get go. Get real!

To accompany someone through the messiness of their faith journey, Pope Francis also offers the following attitudes of accompaniment. Again, my approach here is not to elaborate on each attitude. Instead, I've decided to include, for the purpose of reflection, a quote from Pope Francis for each attitude.

Attitudes of Accompaniment

EMPATHY

And so, with my identity and my empathy, my openness, I walk with the other. I don't try to make him come over to me, I don't proselytize. (POPE FRANCIS, ADDRESS TO BISHOPS OF ASIA, AUGUST 17, 2014)

HUMILITY

In the end, humility means service. It means making room for God by stripping oneself, 'emptying oneself,' as Scripture says. (POPE FRANCIS, PALM SUNDAY HOMILY, MARCH 29, 2015)

SACRIFICE

Holiness means giving ourselves in sacrifice every day. (POPE FRANCIS, TWEET ON MAY 9, 2014)

PATIENCE

With patience: Jesus does not abandon Thomas in his stubborn unbelief; he gives him a week's time, he does not close the door, he waits. And Thomas acknowledges his own poverty, his little faith. "My Lord and my God!": with this simple yet faith-filled invocation, he responds to Jesus' patience. He lets himself be

enveloped by divine mercy; he sees it before his eyes, in the wounds of Christ's hands and feet and in his open side, and he discovers trust: he is a new man, no longer an unbeliever, but a believer.
(POPE FRANCIS, HOMILY, APRIL 7, 2013)

JOY

The joy of the gospel fills the hearts and lives of all who encounter Jesus. Those who accept his offer of salvation are set free from sin, sorrow, inner emptiness and loneliness. With Christ, joy is constantly born anew. (EG, NO. 1)

TENDERNESS

Here I would add one more thing: caring, protecting, demands goodness, it calls for a certain tenderness. In the Gospels, Saint Joseph appears as a strong and courageous man, a working man, yet in his heart we see great tenderness, which is not the virtue of the weak but rather a sign of strength of spirit and a capacity for concern, for compassion, for genuine openness to others, for love. We must not be afraid of goodness, of tenderness. (POPE FRANCIS, HOMILY, MARCH 19, 2013)

OPEN-MINDEDNESS

The centrality of the kerygma [i.e., the gospel message] calls for stressing those elements which are most needed today: it has to express God's saving love which precedes any moral and religious obligation on our part; it should not impose the truth but appeal to freedom; it should be marked by joy, encouragement, liveliness and

a harmonious balance which will not reduce preaching to a few
doctrines which are at times more philosophical than evangelical.
All this demands on the part of the evangelizer certain attitudes
which foster openness to the message: approachability, readiness for
dialogue, patience, a warmth and welcome which is non-
judgmental. (EG, NO. 165)

Now, let's plot these attitudes on our conversion graph.
Remember: (1) *encounter* (2) *sharing faith experiences* (3) *articu-*
lating faith:

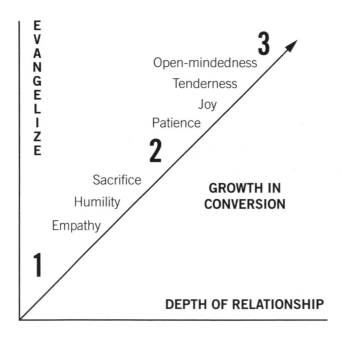

Like the list of accompaniment actions, these attitudes *can* be
reordered. Again, every path of accompaniment is a little dif-

ferent. However, I would submit that the way I have ordered these attitudes gives the evangelizer (companion) the best opportunity for both deepening a relationship with someone while, at the same time, raising the intensity and sophistication level of the evangelization effort and, therefore, deepening the conversion. Let me give my reasons why.

Empathy is listed first, for what I think are obvious reasons. Empathy is that desire and ability to walk in someone else's shoes. In the work of *encounter*, empathy is that attitude which leads us out of ourselves, our world, and into someone else's. Empathy opens the door to others. *Humility* is listed second, but it is necessarily connected with empathy. Humility is that attitude whereby we keep a modest view of ourselves. In other words, the humble person does not seek to exalt himself or herself. Humility is the chief attitude St. Paul uses to describe Jesus and his disciples (Phil 2:1–11). Again, one could argue that humility should come before empathy. However, I placed humility as second because having a modest view of one's self flows from the desire and ability to regard and attend to the lives of others—the ability to put others and their needs first. In other words, empathy opens the door to others, and humility enables us to walk through the doors others open for us.

The attitudes of *sacrifice* and *patience* correspond to the accompaniment phase of *sharing faith experience*. The New Testament understanding of the word "sacrifice" includes the action of offering, which is the way I tend to think about this word. When we share our faith experience(s) with others, we are offering a part of ourselves—a very intimate part—to them. This offering of self includes a degree of vulnerability. When we share our experience of faith, we expose our deepest longings and fears. I placed *patience* at the "halfway point" on the conversion line as a reminder that accompaniment is a marathon, not a sprint. We must pace ourselves for our own sake and for the sake of those we accompany.

Joy, Tenderness, and Open-mindedness are interrelated and belong to the phase of accompaniment known as *articulating faith*. Articulating the faith is not an easy task. When we speak of faith, we are speaking of mysteries. Mysteries are something about which we can have keen, reasonable, and truthful insights; but, ultimately, mystery transcends reason. On this side of the grave, we will never be able to fully comprehend the mysteries of our faith. In light of this, we need to offer the one we are accompanying a joyful disposition, a tender heart, and an open mind, which allow for questions and opposing viewpoints.

One of the things I tell parents to do with their children (keeping age-appropriateness in mind), is to share with them the difficulties they have had understanding and living their faith. You don't have to go to confession to your kids! But there is incredible witness value—incredible power to transform others—when we share our own journey of faith, which includes our successes and failures, our insights and our ignorance. Why do you think St. Augustine's *Confessions* has been one of the most popular Christian devotional reads over millennia? True, he was a theologian of the highest caliber. But more importantly, he was honest about who he was and about the successes and struggles of his own journey of faith. Remember the words from Pope Paul VI I quoted earlier in the book: people today listen more to witnesses than they do to teachers.

Conclusion

Disciples are people who are intentional about the work of accompaniment. The journey of accompaniment is a little different for every person. Some journeys are more linear, and some are "squigglier." The actions and attitudes of accompaniment are guideposts, not rules, to help you companion others in a way that builds relationships that will, in time, be able to bear the weight of the intellectual and emotional difficulties that often come with attempting to understand and incorporate the content of faith into one's lived experience.

FOR REFLECTION

1] Look at the table on p. 64, which lists the actions of accompaniment. When you think about your personal and professional life (or your ministry, if you have one), in which phase of accompaniment are you spending most of your time and energy? Why?

2] Look at the graph on p. 70. Which attitude of accompaniment do you find yourself embodying most frequently? Why?

Chapter Four

Mercy: The Mission of Every Parish

It is absolutely essential for the Church and for the credibility of her message that she herself live and testify to mercy. Her language and her gestures must transmit mercy, so as to touch the hearts of all people and inspire them once more to find the road that leads to the Father. (MV, NO. 12)

The parish is not an outdated institution; precisely because it possesses great flexibility, it can assume quite different contours depending on the openness and missionary creativity of the pastor and the community. While certainly not the only institution which evangelizes, if the parish proves capable of self-renewal and constant adaptivity, it continues to be "the Church living in the midst of the homes of her sons and daughters."...In all its activities the parish encourages and trains its members to be evangelizers. It is a community of communities, a sanctuary where the thirsty come to drink in the midst of their journey, and a center of constant missionary outreach. (EG, NO. 28)

Mission-mindedness

Pope Francis makes it clear that parishes are called to be mission-minded. Being mission-minded translates into *being other-centered*, which includes making meaningful connections with others, building relationships based on trust, respect, and love, and witnessing to the gospel message of mercy in all that we say and do. One might think that being mission-minded is the *de facto* way in which parishes operate, but that isn't true. The recent swell of books focused on discipleship and parish renewal—e.g., *A Community of Disciples* (2012), *Rebuilt* (2012), *Divine Renovation* (2014), and *Becoming a Parish of Intentional Disciples* (2015)—bears out the fact that being missional is not the norm in our parishes.

But what does it mean to be *for others*? Hopefully, if you have read this book from the beginning, you already know the answer. If by chance, however, you are starting at the beginning of this chapter, let me assure you that *being for others*, speaking in the context of evangelization, means *spiritually accompanying others*. Accompaniment—the way of the New Evangelization—turns us outward and focuses our attention and energy on those around us in three major ways: (1) by encounter, (2) by sharing faith experiences, (3) and by articulating faith. Each of these phases of accompaniment includes vital actions and attitudes that support the effort to evangelize and further the conversion process. (For more details, see chapter 3.)

Parish Re-newal Demands "Me-newal"

In a pithy response to a query from the *London Times* (ca. 1908) that read: "What's wrong with the world?" Catholic author G.K. Chesterton wrote: "I am." Decline and renewal, whether in society, culture, or religion, ultimately are brought about through the effort (or lack of effort) on the part of individuals. Likewise, a parish—which is a kind of "mini-society," with its own unique culture—rises or falls based on the decisions and actions (or inaction) of individuals. It follows, then, that *becoming a parish of mercy begins with each individual parishioner's desire and decision to become a companion of others*. This involves a change of mind and heart. Interior change is not usually inspired and cultivated by programs and events but by other people. Evangelization is interpersonal, based on relationships and nurtured by a gradual witness to the gospel message in word and deed. The fact is, before parishes can be renewed, individual relationships must be renewed: introductions come before initiatives, presence before programs, communion before culture change, and witness before watershed moments.

As I stated earlier, this book is for clergy, staff, volunteers, and pew-sitters like me. The intent of this book is to be a thought inspirer and conversation starter. Its message, along with the reflection questions, are meant to be mulled over individually, shared with others, and ultimately lived out. So, rather than offer you, the reader, a program of renewal, I am offering an opportunity for "me-newal." The following is a series of reflections and questions from the perspective of different groups within parish life. These reflections and questions aim to help you prayerfully consider how you might accompany those around you and, therefore, begin becoming a parish of mercy.

Clergy: Both Shepherd and Sheep

Clergy are the leaders of the parish. Leadership, however, takes on many different forms. Pope Francis has offered clergy a leadership-from-behind style, one characterized by humility, transparency/accountability, service, and personal presence to others. The days of the "princely priest" are over. And this is a good thing. This means that clergy, along with everybody else, are called to "take on the smell of the sheep" (EG, no. 24). Clergy are to attend to others and let others attend to them. In this sense, clergy are both shepherds and sheep: they lead others in terms of their role as pastor, presider, celebrant, and catechist. Yet clergy should also be open to being led by those to whom they minister by allowing themselves to receive support and advice, not to mention love, and by embracing a high level of transparency and accountability to the parish.

QUESTIONS FOR REFLECTION

1] How critical to your personal ministry is the work of accompaniment/relationship building?

2] Right now, do you see accompaniment as a key dynamic in the life of your parish? If so, how? If not, why not?

3] When you think about the ways in which the parish forms people (i.e., liturgy, sacramental prep, religious education, adult faith formation, etc.), is building relationships based on respect, trust, and love an obvious element in each of these areas? Why or why not?

4] Using the language of the actions and attitudes of accompaniment (pp. 64, 70), identify one way in which you could accompany your staff more intentionally. How about those involved in parish ministry? Or the people in the pews? Or those who do not come to your parish?

5] Leadership is as much about leading as it is the willingness to be led. In what ways do you see yourself leading others? In what ways are you willing to let yourself be led by others?

Parish Staff: The Neck that Turns the Head

Where would any parish be without its staff, even when that "staff" is only one person? Like pastors, parish staff have the important work of being the face of the Father's mercy for people. When it comes to parish administration, I have found that folks tend to view this role as vital to the parish but in a secular sense. Many see administrative work as merely "pushing papers"—balancing budgets, tracking sacramental records, and keeping the parish schedule (and Father) organized. While these functions are included, "administration"—which, by the way, is derived from the word "minister"—can contribute greatly to becoming a parish of mercy.

Administrators are often the face of the parish when it comes to new members or when people desire to receive a sacrament or when it is time to commend a loved one to God. Each of these examples provides an excellent opportunity for administrators to be a reflection of God's mercy, to be an open door (and, sometimes, to open the door) for others! First encounters are critical; they help to begin cultivating a credible witness to the gospel message alive in the parish community. First impressions matter. If I walk into the parish office and I see what looks like a smaller version of the IRS, and I am treat-ed as such, my impression of the parish will not be very positive. By working on the front lines, meeting and greeting everyone who comes to the parish doors, by helping to keep the clergy and community organized and moving forward, and by all the various functions they perform, parish staff provide critical support to the overall ministry and life of the parish. Staff members too are called to be companions.

QUESTIONS FOR REFLECTION

1] Do you think of yourself as the "face of the parish," as a person involved in the work of accompaniment? Why? Why not?

2] Thinking of the different phases of accompaniment and their corresponding actions (p. 65), where do find yourself spending most of your time and energy? Why?

3] Looking at the various attitudes of accompaniment (p. 70), which do you find yourself adopting the most? Why?

4] Using the language of the actions and attitudes, identify one way you could accompany Father and others on staff more intentionally. How about the people in the pews, or those who do not attend your parish?

Lay Ministers: Co-Workers in the Vineyard

This title hearkens back to a document produced by the United States Conference of Catholic Bishops (USCCB) titled, *Co-Workers in the Vineyard of the Lord: A Resource for Guiding the Development of Lay Ecclesial Ministry* (2005). A landmark document, *Co-Workers* laid the groundwork for the development and execution of parish lay ministry. Parish ministry is multifaceted: it is pastoral, administrative, sacramental, communal, service-oriented, and catechetical. Lay ministers are called to bring their gifts and talents to bear in each of these categories, always in support of the clergy, and never for their own sakes.

One of the greatest dangers facing lay ministry in the parish today is the tendency for various ministries to become "silos." It is often the case in parish ministry that each ministry feels it is responsible for its portion of "grain" only—its portion of the parish's overall ministry and life. In a parish intent on becoming more merciful, all parish ministries, no matter how unique, have the same task: sharing the gospel message. And we know that relationships rooted in respect, trust, and love are the bedrock of evangelization. Therefore, effective lay ministry of any kind begins with encounter—the forming of relationships based on respect, trust, and love—and attends to the other phases of accompaniment. Ministry will either succeed or fail based on how well ministers can accompany each other.

Jesus once said, "If a house is divided against itself, that house will not be able to stand" (Mk 3:25). The parish is a local expression and experience of God's house, the Church. If a parish's ministries are functioning as silos, irrespective of each other, or if particular ministries function regardless of their constituents, the house soon begins to collapse. And this collapse is felt in terms of apathy and attrition on the part of parishioners. Lay ministry, like clerical ministry, must be focused on the work of accompaniment.

QUESTIONS FOR REFLECTION

1] How do you see your ministry as involving the work of accompaniment?

2] What is one action of accompaniment (p. 64) that you would like to execute more intentionally? How will you do this?

3] What is one attitude of accompaniment (p. 70) that you would like to adopt more intentionally? How will you do this?

4] Inter-ministerial collaboration can mean a lot of things (e.g., sharing calendars, participating in parish staff meetings, co-coordinating parish events, etc.). What else might "collaboration" need to mean so that your particular ministry might avoid becoming a silo?

5] In what ways do you (or might you better) accompany parish clergy and/or staff?

6] In what ways do you (or might you better) accompany the person in the pew and/or the non-church goer?

Pew-Sitters: From Filling Seats to Filling Hearts

I have used the term "pew-sitter" in this book as a way to describe the average parishioner, which includes myself. At my parish, I have a tendency to be a seat-filler and not much more. Now, I am not judging anyone here. Everyone has their reasons why they are (or are not) involved in their parish. Truthfully, I am not advocating that everyone be involved in a parish ministry of sorts. Accompaniment belongs to every arena of life. What I am advocating for is a change of mind and heart, a renewal from within (Rom 12:2). Becoming a parish of mercy does not begin in the parish office; it begins in the pews. And it begins with the work of encounter. A former Baptist minister and current colleague of mine tells me that parishioners at his parish typically do not know how to care for each other, or even that they are called to do so.

Now, the level of "parish care" can be both defined and measured in a variety of ways. Doing so, however, would go beyond the scope of this book. Yet I do think my friend is on to something. I can honestly say, based on my own experience as a Catholic who has worked either in parish or diocesan ministry in four different dioceses, that being attentive to others—their presence, their personal needs, their importance to us, personally, and to the larger community—is not something that comes naturally to most parishes. Most of us have to fight the tendency to be individualists: people who focus only on themselves and their own rights, needs, and desires.

For example, from the moment my family walks into the church for Sunday Mass to the moment we leave, it is a struggle for me to be attentive to those around me. And by "attentive" I mean "being aware" of and personally engaging others beyond my family. Typically, I am thinking about what my children need, or I am keeping them from jumping off the pews or having staring contests with the people in the pew behind us. Or I am often thinking about what I need, what the word of God means to me today or the things I need to pray for. And let me be clear: these are all good things. However, to help my parish become more merciful—more of a sacramental people for others—I need to play my part. I need to go out of myself, go out of my comfort zone, be attentive to and engage the body of Christ that is around me (1 Cor 11:18–30).

I said that mercy, in general, is an orientation toward the other; and that, consequently, a parish of mercy is one in which people come first. Pew-sitters, by far, make up the majority of every parish. In fact, I can't even imagine a parish that has more clergy, more staff, or more lay ministers than overall parishioners. Therefore, one can imagine that becoming a parish of mercy happens largely due to the efforts of individual pew-sitters like me—people who, one day, decide to plug into their parish and/or into the lives of those around them in a way that moves from encounter to deep faith sharing.

If you haven't noticed, becoming a parish of mercy is the accumulation of a lot of little acts of mercy done on the part of individuals—as Blessed Mother Teresa famously said, what matters are "little acts done with great love." The pew-sitter has so many opportunities in front of him or her to put the actions and attitudes of accompaniment to work—in the parish, at home, at work, or in the larger community. There are only two questions that need answering: First, do I want to be a companion? And second, how might I be called to be one? For the pew-sitter, the call to accompany is fluid and spontaneous, probably more so than for the parish minister, staff member, or clergy. And because of this, it requires a keen sense of discernment and a true desire to be an open door for others—that through you others may encounter "the Father of Mercies" (2 Cor 1:3). Discernment begins with desire. Do you have the desire to accompany others? If not, pray for that desire! An old Franciscan friend once said to me, when I had little-to-no desire to pray, "You need to pray for the desire to desire to pray." Huh? What? And then I understood: desire is not something we manufacture. Like anything else in the spiritual life, desire is a grace. Sometimes we have to ask for it. And sometimes we even have to beg!

QUESTIONS FOR REFLECTION

1] How might you practice the art of accompaniment in your home? Your workplace? Your parish?

2] What is one action of accompaniment (p. 64) you would like to execute more intentionally? How will you do this?

3] What is one attitude of accompaniment (p. 70) you would like to adopt more intentionally? How will you do this?

4] How might you accompany the clergy, staff, or lay ministers of your parish? Think: "little actions done with great love."

Conclusion

We need constantly to contemplate the mystery of mercy. It is a wellspring of joy, serenity, and peace. Our salvation depends on it. Mercy: the word reveals the very mystery of the Most Holy Trinity. Mercy: the ultimate and supreme act by which God comes to meet us. Mercy: the fundamental law that dwells in the heart of every person who looks sincerely into the eyes of his brothers and sisters on the path of life. Mercy: the bridge that connects God and man, opening our hearts to the hope of being loved forever despite our sinfulness. (MV, NO. 2)

It would be unfortunate if, after reading this book, you, the reader, use it *only* as a way to acknowledge, celebrate, and live the Jubilee Year of Mercy (2015-2016). Don't get me wrong; those are all good things! But as the above quote points out, mercy is more than a theme or motif. Mercy speaks to the very nature of God; and, because we are made in God's image and likeness, merciful is what we are called to be. Mercy is the heart of the gospel message, and how we share that message ought to reflect this truth. Finally, mercy is the way of Christian perfection. If you aren't sure about that last statement, let me offer a quick Bible study.

Have you ever compared the Sermon on the Mount (Matthew, chapters 5—7) with the Sermon on the Plain (Luke 6:17–49)? While there are many similarities between the two, there are also noticeable differences. In particular, one notices a difference in tone. In Matthew's version, Jesus speaks in idealistic and somewhat abstract terms, whereas Luke's version is more practical and down-to-earth. For example, let's compare Mt 5:48 with Lk 6:36, which also illustrates my earlier point—that mercy is the way of Christian perfection.

In both versions of Jesus' sermon, Mt 5:48 and Lk 6:36 represent a moment of climax. In Matthew's version, Jesus says to the crowd, "So be perfect as your heavenly father is perfect." This is no small feat! So, immediately, we ask the question: How can God expect me to be perfect? It doesn't seem possible. This is because, for many, being "perfect" translates into being "sinless"—or having arrived at a state in life whereby one only commits "small" sins. Actually, the word "perfect," here, translates from the biblical Greek into "completeness," "lacking nothing," "mature," and/or "reaching the end or goal."

Reading Luke's version of the sermon, we are given a practical example of what Jesus means by perfection. Here, Jesus does not repeat the exhortation/command to "be perfect" found in Matthew's version. Rather, Jesus says, "Be *merciful*, just as your Father is *merciful* [italics mine]." Putting the two versions together, we come to see that *to be perfect is to be merciful*. In other words, to live "perfectly" is to live a full, mature Christian life; and, in light of Luke's gospel, this means that we are called to live a life full of mercy: receiving and sharing mercy with others. Is there any greater news than this?

The gospel message is a call to mercy. The gospels proclaim God—as revealed in and through Jesus of Nazareth—to be merciful beyond compare, beyond one's wildest imagination. This is why the gospels are good news in the first place! In addition, the gospel message is a call to encounter, to relationship with God, whereby people experience mercy as the love, gift, and liberation of God, promised through his only son, Jesus Christ. The work of the parish of mercy is to facilitate this encounter and to foster in others a relationship with God by cultivating, both collectively and individually, the attitudes and actions of accompaniment.

I began this book by saying that *God draws straight with crooked lines*. Crooked lines are only straightened when we, like God, accompany others along their curvy, twisty paths.

And why is this so? Because, when we accompany others, we bring the kingdom of God to them, right where they are on their journey. And where the kingdom is, there our home is also, the destination of our journey. I hope, through this book, to accompany you [and your parish] as, together, we build parishes of mercy.

> *Mercy is the heart of God. It must also be the heart of the members of the one great family of his children: a heart which beats all the more strongly wherever human dignity—as a reflection of the face of God in his creatures—is in play. Jesus tells us that love for others—foreigners, the sick, prisoners, the homeless, even our enemies—is the yardstick by which God will judge our actions. Our eternal destiny depends on this.… This then is why "it is absolutely essential for the Church and for the credibility of her message that she herself live and testify to mercy. Her language and her gestures must transmit mercy, so as to touch the hearts of all people and inspire them once more to find the road that leads to the Father."*
>
> (POPE FRANCIS, MESSAGE FOR THE CELEBRATION OF XLIX WORLD DAY OF PEACE, JANUARY 1, 2016)